Customer Profitability Analytics

A practical guide to
methods and technologies

By Dave McNab, CPA, CA

Copyright Notice

Bibliographic reference:

McNab, Dave (2015) <u>Customer Profitability Analytics: A practical guide to methods and technologies.</u> Toronto, Ontario, Canada: Objective Business Services Inc.

For educational use please contact the author for permission to reproduce or redistribute to your students at http://www.objectivebusiness.com.

Table of Contents

What is Customer Profitability and why should we measure it?

Preamble

There's no place to start like the beginning, and these questions (what and why) are certainly the right place to begin when you need to decide whether or not your business should be investing in measurement of customers' profitability.

Let's start with the first one: what is Customer profitability? The obvious answer is that it is how much a customer contributes to your company's profit. What this really means in practice, however, seems to get complicated in a hurry as soon as we start to look a little more closely what we've just said.

What is a Customer?

Before spending a dime on customer profitability (or relationship based marketing in general for that matter) it makes a whole lot of sense to figure out who your customers are. And believe it or not, Customer likely means different things to different people within your company.

For example: within a Canadian retail bank a customer might mean an account holder; the originator of a transaction, an individual, a household or a family. Depending on who in the organization we ask, we may hear very different views about who or what a customer is.

There may also be complexities in the nature of the relationship between your company and your customers. Joint ownership and multiple beneficiaries of accounts (especially in business to business relationships) add complexity to the question. Intermediaries that play a bridging role between company and end customer, for example the relationship between Insurance provider and broker pose challenges to a simple notion of customer.

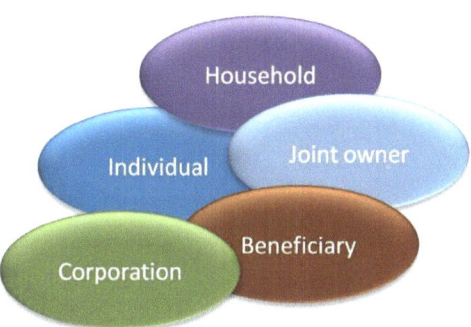

So it is evident that we had best figure out what we mean by "Customer" before we get started. To offer some guidance on this rather thorny issue we suggest this guideline: a customer should be a purchasing decision unit. What this means in the context of your business may require some careful thought.

Once you have defined who your customers are, the next issue that pops up is whether or not you can actually recognize them in your data. You need the ability to say which transactions and accounts relate to a given customer or you cannot achieve an actionable view of their behavior and it's implication for profitability of your company. This is usually achieved by establishing a customer hierarchy within your database.

Creating a customer hierarchy is a technical issue, usually resolved by building a Customer Information File (CIF) which cross references customers – however defined - to accounts and transactions. Many companies use Householding algorithms to achieve a similar matching of customers to business activity. Both CIF development and Householding methods are substantial topics that we will leave to a separate discussion. Suffice it to say that it is very difficult to proceed without a reliable customer hierarchy if you want to measure customer profitability.

What is Profitability?

Now that the foundation is established we get into the next big question: what is profit anyway? Again there is an obvious answer - it is revenue minus expenses. But which revenues and which expenses to include and when to include them is not at all clear when we take a closer look at your customers' behavior and your business.

Should revenue be recognized when it is received (cash basis) or when it is earned (accrual basis)? Should your existing customers bear the cost of money spent on soliciting new business from someone else? Which customers should bear the cost of corporate functions like the Lear Jet? Should insurance claim experience or loan losses, or warranty claims or coupons be attributed to individuals (and when)?

Figure 2: What is profitability?

These are not trivial or easy questions to answer. The decisions you make concerning the treatment of individual revenue and expense items will have profound impact on the absolute profitability measurement results and the relative profit ranking of your customers. For example one Canadian bank learned that using average cost per account instead of individual transaction costs changed the ranking of many of its customers by three deciles or more. Their experience highlights how important it is to build a measurement that truly reflects your business.

Once your accounting methods are figured out are we done? Not really. There are other questions you should think about as well to ensure that the measurement you are going to build will support the decisions you need to make in your business.

In some businesses it is imperative to measure the profitability of customers in relation to the capital resources they consume (e.g. Return on Capital for a lending business). In others it is important to measure profitability over the duration of a cycle that is inherent in the business (e.g. lifetime of a car lease, a growing season for a farmer, a project lifetime for a building contractor, a redemption cycle for a loyalty program customer). There are a wide variety of measurements that may be used to provide insight into the profitability of your customers' business. Choosing what to measure and how will profoundly affect the usefulness of the information you produce.

Customer Profitability measurement is not the simplest thing to implement, yet many leading companies have surmounted the challenges that it presents. Why would you want to go through the effort of figuring all this out and building (or buying) a system to do it?

Why we should measure it?

We willingly admit to having a bias towards measuring customer profitability: at a basic level we believe that what gets measured gets managed. Managing value exchanges with your customers as a strategic process is just as relevant now as it was when CRM was first touted as the next great thing. What Customer Profitability adds to the mix is an understanding of what pays and what doesn't.

Managing Sales

We were once asked to revamp the compensation program for a commissioned sales force. At the time the 100 or so sales people were generating a substantial negative net present value to the company. The solution we developed was to retarget the sales on which commissions were paid: the rate of commission was built on a sliding scale related to the profitability of the business generated. The result was a turn-around from loss to profit to the tune several million dollars a year (NPV). At the heart of the analysis was an understanding of customer profitability.

In another example related by a fellow council member a retail bank found the discounts demanded by one customer drove their profitability so far into the negative ($40,000 on $10 million in deposits) that they were actually better off letting the customer go elsewhere. Situations like this occur across many different industries where customers negotiate prices.

Sales effectiveness is best monitored through a combination of activity measurements and results measurements. Activity measurements are needed to promote productivity and identify actions that can be taken to improve individual performance. As Tom Peters would say this is about "doing the thing right".

Results measurement is needed to ensure that our sales people are doing "the right thing". Historically we have spent lots of time effort and money acquiring business that provides low or negative value to our companies. The classic statistic first uncovered in Retail Banking is that 80% of their client base is at or below the zero profit mark. As measurement of customer profitability has spread, we hear similar findings echoed in a number of different industries.

It is quite clear that acquiring profitable customers is a key to managing the margin and the bottom line of your business. Without a disciplined analysis of the profitability of your existing client base it is very difficult to tell which types of customers you should be identifying for acquisition. All of the other target marketing information you presently use remains valid and useful: the difference is you learn which customers you want to acquire.

Having knowledge of customer profitability enables your company to manage and compensate the sales function for delivering value to the organization, rather than revenue or unit sales.

Managing Service

To avoid entering into a debate over the difference between sales and service here please allow us to define service as providing fulfillment of the sales promise to your customers. Each industry is different in the way it provides service to customers but it is invariably an activity that provides value to your customers and cost to your organization. One of the key issues in managing service is the allocation of costly resources to customer service rationally.

For example, one Canadian energy services company established a policy of increasing the general level of reserved service "black-out" periods to create capacity. This enabled reallocation of their trucks and technicians to more rapidly service their best customers without increasing overall cost.

Understanding customer profitability offers a myriad of opportunities to you for managing the effectiveness of the resource allocation decisions you make concerning service. In Canada many industries have a bias towards providing all customers with equality of service levels. While this is one of the cultural attributes that makes us Canadian, it is absurd from a business perspective. Not all customers offer the same value to our companies. Why then must we provide the same service to all customers? The answer may be complex in a regulated industry or one with a high public profile or public purpose, but in many for-profit corporations there is really no good reason that service differentiation cannot or should not be implemented.

Service differentiation opens up the potential to treat your best customers better and to save money by reducing the levels of service provided to customers who contribute less to your company's well being. Remember that there is a numbers game going on here: it is possible to reduce service level 10% on 80% of the customer base and increase it 40% for the remainder for the same cost.

Altering service levels can take many forms. It may involve alterations in reward and recognition program premiums; call wait periods; access to privileged locations, times or content; face time with staff; fast-track processing or just about anything else you can think of that might be valuable to your preferred customers.

The key to affecting service level decisions is knowing two things: who you are affecting and how much change you can afford. Measuring customer profitability can help you to answer both of those questions with facts.

Managing Product

Product management is as necessary a discipline in a customer centric organization as it ever has been. Product managers have usually been blessed with access to some form of product profitability measurement which informs their management processes and thinking. Consequently we rarely see product managers emerging as the proponents of customer profitability in companies. We think this is unfortunate, as there is indeed opportunity lurking in this information for the product manager too.

What the customer view brings to them is a deeper understanding of product interdependencies from a customer perspective. It is no longer appropriate to look at a pricing decision or a product add / drop decision strictly on the basis of the individual product's profitability. Management of customer value demands that we also consider which of our customers are using the products or services we are making these decisions about.

Where are the opportunities to optimize loss leaders for our preferred customers? Where can we create an opportunity for holistic relationship pricing? How much can we afford to give as discounts – to whom? Where can we raise prices without risking our key customers? What are the implications for new product development? These are the kind of questions our product managers need to be considering.

Managing Operations
Operations management is largely concerned with optimizing processes to achieve efficiency and effectiveness. This management challenge inevitably results in substantial change as new technologies and practices are adopted.

One of the several insights that customer profitability can provide is to highlight which customers are affected by changes and the risk that the organization is taking by implementing operational changes. This is critical when evaluating risk and when making communications to customers about changes the company is implementing.

Another important way that customer profitability can be used in operations is in the evaluation of which processes and procedures are adding value to the company. For example, processes which involve few of the higher end customers have lower value than those that support large numbers of high end customers. Ultimately operations processes can and should be measured in relation to customers and customer value.

Managing Finance

In my years as a Financial Controller I was always amused by the budget setting process. It seemed to be a tug-of-war between the conservative projections of management and the Board which always demanded a far higher return. In the end I always found the resultant plans to be somewhat dissatisfying, sort of like a cease fire called because we ran out of time for the war.

Did we have the kind of information we really needed? What would happen if the Board said the objective was to "close the gap between current value and potential value by 10% and add 5% to revenue from net new business"? With customer profitability measurement this kind of objectives based business planning becomes possible. It also gives a much clearer direction to management than traditional planning measures.

In our experience customer profitability information has not yet taken on this level of strategic use in Finance. This may be because the measures are relatively new, and adoption takes time. Nonetheless we foresee that this is where business planning is inevitably going to head, because the customer really is the central measurement basis for your company. Your company's present value is the sum of the present values of your customers. Your company's potential value is the sum of the potential value of your customers plus a factor for net new business. In many business acquisitions these are now taken into account as critical factors in the valuation process. Knowing what these values are is central to understanding the real value of your business franchise.

Conclusion

Customer profitability measurement is challenging to implement; it draws into question our understanding of who our customers are and how we make profit.

It can add powerful insights throughout your business, helping to focus decision making energies on doing what is right for your customers and your shareholders at the same time. In a customer centric organization, measuring customer profitability has become a business imperative: without it there is no fact basis for managing the value exchange between your company and your customers.

Our sense is that you can ill afford to manage without these facts as you make decisions concerning the sales, service, product management, operations and finance functions of your business... especially if your competitors have them.

How should we measure Customer Profitability?

In the previous article in this series we discussed what customer profitability is and some of the key benefits of measuring it. We argued that you can ill afford to manage without this information as you make decisions concerning the sales, service, product management, operations and finance functions of your business.

In this article we bring the discussion down to a more concrete level, exploring the measurement issues you are likely to encounter in the design of a customer profitability measurement "formula". We talk about these issues in the context of business decisions, because the appropriate measurement method depends on what question you are trying to answer. Unlike public financial reporting, where accounting rules are prescribed, customer profitability measurement is management information. There are no set rules that have to be followed. The choice of accounting methods depends on the information needs of internal decision makers.

To build a model that will meet your needs, you need to understand the relationship between the types of decisions you make and the accounting choices that have to be made when building a measurement model. If you don't consider these factors you run the risk of (a) building an expensive model that doesn't help you run the business or even worse (b) making misinformed business decisions that have a direct impact on your customers.

Types of decisions

Customer profitability can be useful to inform decision making in many contexts. Regardless of where responsibility lies within your organization, decisions are made routinely in which the value exchange between customer and company is being changed. Measuring customer profitability gives you insight into the effects of these changes and offers you the opportunity to manage them.

Some of the proactive decisions that marketing managers face every day deal with the allocation of resources, specifically things like:

- Choosing which prospective customers to acquire
- Choosing which customers you want to retain
- Choosing which customers to cross-sell (and what to sell them)
- Choosing which customers you may want to abandon
- Choosing channels of distribution
- Setting the price (or discount structure) for a product or service
- Setting sales compensation rates
- Setting reward program entitlements
- Setting advertising and promotion budgets
- Setting service levels for customers
- Identifying customer behaviors that create or destroy value

In addition to making these proactive choices, we also want to know what kind of results we are producing. Customer profitability can provide us insight into key performance metrics like:

- Measuring the cost of lost business
- Measuring the value of new business
- Return on a campaign
- Return on an offer
- Return on a pricing change
- Return on changes in service delivery

Bases of measurement l: Time dimension

There are four primary measurements of customer value that can be used to help us answer these questions.

Historical value of a customer looks at the value earned from a customer relationship over an extended period of time, such as prior fiscal quarter, prior year or since the start of the relationship. It can be measured as a simple average of previous periods or can be time weighted, placing higher emphasis on recent periods. Averaging in this manner has the effect of smoothing reported results for a customer, lending consistency to the reported values. Historical value is most useful for comparing customers with each other in order to rank them, selecting groups for marketing efforts and for assessing pricing or budgeting decisions.

Current value looks to a shorter time frame, often a month (in order to coincide with reporting cycles). Current value is often volatile, since cyclical factors in the relationship are often not reflected within a single month. Current value has the advantage of highlighting the effects of changes in the customer relationship when compared to previous period current values. It is most useful for quantifying the benefit of campaigns, new offers, and pricing changes on customer value.

Present value is a future oriented measurement, which typically considers the future revenue and cost streams of the customer's existing business. This measure is usually only extended to include the contractual lifetime of ongoing products or services. Revenues and costs are projected into the future using essentially the same methods as in current value and then are discounted to the present using a discount rate appropriate to the business (for example the cost of capital). Present value is useful for ranking customers according to value, determining sales compensation rates, and is frequently used as a basis for modeling the impact of decisions concerning price and service before they are implemented. A comparison of present value of customers between time periods also provides a sound basis for evaluating program results for marketing campaigns.

Lifetime value is another future oriented measurement, again based on the same methods that are used in current value measurement. What distinguishes it from present value is a modeling component: lifetime value takes into account projected revenue and cost streams not only from the existing relationship but also from business that is expected to be done with the customer in the future. To implement lifetime value a company must have a substantial insight into renewal or repurchase behavior and propensity of the customer to add or reduce the extent of their business relationship in the future. The projected cash flows are usually discounted in a manner similar to present value. Lifetime value is often viewed as the optimal customer value measurement for most decision making situations. Unfortunately few companies have the experience and models required to produce a lifetime value measurement that management is comfortable with.

Figure 3: Historical, Current, Present and Lifetime Value

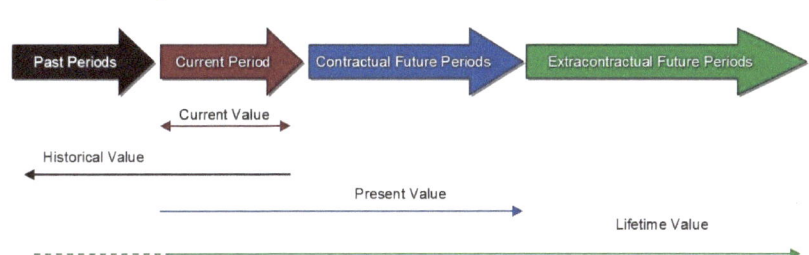

There are different measurements for different purposes, and variations in precision levels that can be attained. In an unlimited resources situation, we would provide management with all of them. Best in class customer profitability systems today support all of these measures. Implementation is primarily limited by the available data, models and resources of the company that is implementing the technology solution.

Starting out, most companies strive to implement a credible current value measurement. Under ideal circumstances this can be extended backwards in time to encompass historical information, generating multi-period results in the first release of the system (six or twelve months of history is usually the best that can be done practically).

From this base of current value history the next step is usually implementation of historical value. Present value and lifetime value are more sophisticated measurements and are usually implemented as a later upgrade to customer profitability information after the organization has gained experience working with the new information provided by current and historical measurements.

Bases of measurement II: Accounting theories

Regardless of which bases of measurement are selected, there are a number of technical accounting issues which will need to be addressed when tailoring the calculations to fit your business. In this section we will explore some of the major decisions that need to be made, looking at revenue, cost, and finally probabilistic items like insurance claims, coupon redemptions and loan losses.

As a Marketing professional you may not view accounting as an area of personal interest or expertise, and you may be inclined to delegate determination of accounting treatments to the Finance department. This is not always a good idea: the way customer profitability is calculated may need to be different than accounting profitability measurement in order to be useful for marketing purposes. For example consider account closing costs: from a financial accounting perspective they cannot be included until the account closes. From a marketing perspective, however, we need to include these costs during the lifetime of the account when we are setting prices. This type of conflict needs careful resolution when designing how your customer profitability calculations will work.

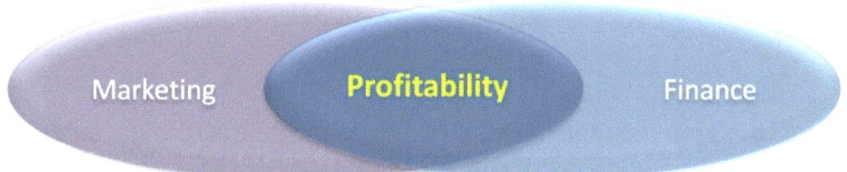

Another consideration is the degree of precision that you need to have in order for the measurement to be useful for marketing purposes. If you are sponsoring development of the measurement you certainly have a voice concerning how far your company should go to make the measurement reflect all revenue and cost items fully. In some industries it may be appropriate to simply measure revenue or revenue minus some simple costs (such as cost of goods sold) to provide information which adequately identifies the relative profitability of customers. In this article we contemplate a more sophisticated – and complex – model in order to make the discussion more universal. Your knowledge of your business will ultimately determine how much detail and precision needs to be included in your own customer profitability measurement.

If you want to have a useful customer profitability system, you will probably need to work with Finance as your partner to provide expertise defining the requirements that will be implemented and to help resolve these types of conflicts.

Revenue

The main choice that needs to be made concerning revenue is whether you want to recognize it on a Cash basis or an Accrual basis.

If you were to account for revenue on a cash basis, revenue from each customer would be recognized when the money received from them is banked. This is typically pretty simple – we usually would ignore small differences in timing caused by credit card payments and cheques, recognizing sales at the time the sale transaction is settled. On this basis revenue is essentially recognized when the cash register rings or invoices are produced.

Revenue

Accrual basis, on the other hand, attempts to match the recognition of revenue with the costs that relate to generating it. This can cut two ways: it is possible to defer revenue (recognize it in the future) when payment is received in advance of services being provided, it is also possible to accrue revenue (recognize it in the present) when services are provided in advance of payment. For example an annual fee could be spread over the year it relates to: either before it is received (if paid in arrears) or after it is received (if it is paid in advance).

In some industries this is a big deal. In Construction, Franchising and Banking for instance there are special rules indicating how to treat certain items of revenue laid down by accounting authorities. The accounting rules for financial reporting have a bias towards conservatism, however, that may be inappropriate for your customer profitability model. For example, accounting rule makers are very keen on deferring revenue but they are less inclined towards accruing revenue (since that can be used to inflate profit).

As a general rule accrual accounting provides a smoother recognition of profit in any given period, and is desirable for any purpose other than management of cash flow or business valuation. Most companies will choose to adopt an accrual basis of accounting for customer revenue. As you go through analysis of the types of revenue that occur in your business along with Finance you need to make sure that the treatment of revenue is as good an approximation of the business as is possible – even if it differs from your Finance policies. Remember that you are creating a management information measurement not a financial reporting system.

Cost

Costing is always a thorny issue. In most companies we see there are concerns that costing is not accurate enough, is not complete or is stale. This in itself is not a show-stopper when you want to build a customer profitability measurement. Most leading companies which have implemented customer profitability measurements do so using what costing information they have available, and then identify areas for future improvement, working with Finance to set the agenda for costing work. This can actually be a big win for the Finance function, as it drives relevance and direction (and even funding) in the process of costing.

Costs in a customer profitability model may include transaction-specific amounts or customer-specific amounts. Transaction-specific costs would include such things as the cost of a product purchased, opening an account or conducting a sale. Customer-specific costs may include such items as the cost of producing a customer statement, direct mail marketing or credit approval. Indirect costs are things like corporate overheads that are hard to relate to customers or transactions.

The ABC's of Costing

When Finance prepares costing information, they usually use a method called Activity-Based Costing (ABC). In that process they identify activities which combine to produce products or services (often both internal and external). Using time and motion studies and analyzing the use of resources, they determine the cost of performing an activity, and then determine the cost of various products and services.

When preparing ABC, it is common for costs to be identified as direct (caused by the activity, like cost of goods sold) or indirect (required for the activity to happen, like the cost of rent in a store) and also to have some fairly large chunks of cost dollars that remain unallocated to activities. It is also common to distinguish between fixed costs (those that do not change substantially with sales volume, like rent) and variable costs (which do, like cost of goods sold).

One of the decisions you need to make is whether to include all of these components. Direct variable costs are useful when making decisions at the margin (next customer, next unit) such as a negotiated price decision. For most product and customer management decisions, you will likely want to have a fuller inclusion of costs, usually direct and indirect, including both fixed and variable components. These less direct costs and particularly those of a fixed nature will require allocation to customers on some basis that will not distort the ranking of customers. Inclusion of unallocated costs is needed if you wish to be able to reconcile back to the financial records of the company – a requirement in many implementations of customer profitability.

So what to do? We believe it is a good idea, when practical, to include both fixed and variable direct, indirect and allocated costs in the customer profitability model. Best practice is to store these levels of cost inclusion as separate subtotals of total cost, so that reporting can be based on a level of cost inclusion appropriate to the decisions which are being considered.

Accrual versus Cash

As with revenue there are issues concerned with timing associated with cost, and the decisions you make will be affected by the same logic: it is generally desirable to match revenue and expense regardless of when they actually happen. Again there is a bias among the accounting authorities towards conservatism that you should be aware of. Accounting authorities are keen on accruing costs but they are less inclined to permit deferral (since that can be used to inflate profit). In general accrual which matches revenue and expense flows as closely as possible is what we should want in our customer profitability model.

Bases of Costing

There are other issues which we also have to look at for costs. Over the years we have developed a number of bases for measuring costs which are specifically useful for different circumstances. Determining the basis of costing to be used in your customer profitability model is important as it will have a significant impact on the actual results you produce. The three main costing bases you need to know about and consider are Actual cost, Standard Cost, Average cost.

Actual cost measures the cost of actually performing a transaction, making a product, taking a phone call or some other activity. Costs on this basis are usually determined by taking the expenses of the company and allocating them to activities. Actual cost is helpful for understanding the real profit of customers, products etc. taking into account efficiencies resulting from variances in day to day operations. Unfortunately actual cost data is hard to get on a timely basis, since it can only be determined after the books are closed. For customer profitability we usually need something that is available faster to reflect the competitive urgency of the decisions we need to make.

Standard cost measures the cost of an activity according to an attainable performance standard. Costs on this basis are determined by process engineers who identify how the activity should be done and the value of resources that should be consumed to do it. Standard costs do not change from month to month. Standard cost is helpful when volumes are highly variable, especially in a product launch situation, where it would distort profitability to reflect the actual cost base over a small volume of activity.

Average cost most often allocates actual costs (from an earlier accounting period) to a customer-related cost driver such as account without reference to the activity level of the individual customer. Typically this method is used when behavioral cost drivers (activity data) are not available. To some extent it is necessary to use average costs to deal with unallocated costs in a customer profitability model. In the absence of ABC costing, average cost is often used in first implementations. This method of costing is generally inadequate for customer value management purposes. In the Retail Banking industry in Canada, for instance, dramatic shifts in customer profitability have been noted when changing from average cost per account to a more behavior sensitive measurement using historical or standard cost.

Probabilistic items

In many businesses it is not possible to foresee the amount of cost that may be incurred in the future because an event may or may not happen in the future. This is a widespread issue dealing with probabilistic things such as the likelihood a coupon will be cashed, of a car accident claim, of a loan default or of goods being returned for credit. It crops up in almost any business.

The first thing we should consider if you have items like these is how important they are to the overall numbers. If the amounts involved are small, you may be better off ignoring them.

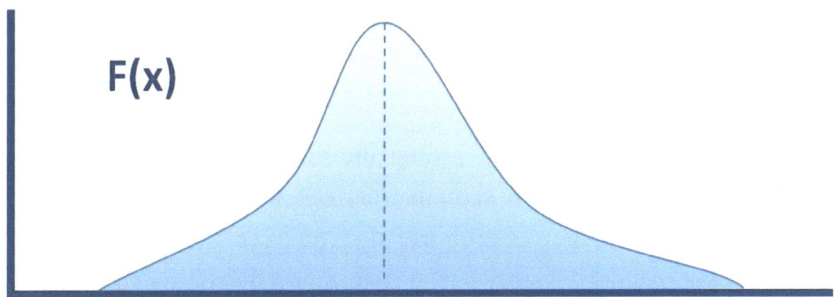

If you decide that you need to take them into account, the next decision is whether you want to attribute the cost to an individual directly (for example a mail-in rebate might be tagged to an individual) or whether you want to take a portfolio approach to the probability of the cost and spread it over the entire relevant customer base (for example allowing for a percentage of credit card balances to go into default). This is a something that is very specific to your business and needs to be decided internally.

If you need to make provisions for probabilistic future costs you will need to identify both the expected amount of the cost (difficult for car accident claims!) and the likelihood that it will happen. Both of these factors can usually be determined with reference to historical data. Once you have determined the probability it will happen and the expected amount it will cost, you will need to translate that expected cost (e.g. probability X amount) into an amount that you wish to attribute each measurement period (e.g. monthly cost = expected cost/ account lifetime in months), and determine a basis for allocating that amount to your customers.

An Illustration

To illustrate this process consider loan losses in a bank. You know that you will have some losses and you know some customers are more at risk than others, but you don't know how much will be lost, when or on which specific loan customers. Unfortunately it is also a big dollar item so it can't be ignored. So what do banks do?

First they recognize that the amount at risk is specific to each individual loan, depending on the amount of the loan, its insurance status and any collateral that backs the loan up as security. This solves the problem of estimating, at the account level, how much could be lost.

The second step is to identify the probability of default. This is done using, among other things, credit risk scoring of individual customers. Other considerations like the type of property pledged as collateral and the type of loan and the payment history of the customer may also be considered. Banks mine their historical data to determine historical probability of default for their customers based on factors such as these.

The next step is to identify the periodic charge for expected loss that should be reflected on the account. This is done with reference to the life of the loan itself, to ensure that when all the periodic charges are added up it equals the amount at risk times the probability of default (the total expected loss). Since all of these factors are tied specifically to an individual customer and their account, there is a high degree of precision in the allocation of these costs to individual customers.

Loan loss estimation in a Bank is both mature science and sophisticated because of the mission critical nature of the cost. In most industries a less sophisticated analysis (using a similar framework, however) will prove adequate for measurement of indeterminate items.

Mapping decisions to accounting theories

If you are going to implement a Customer Profitability Measurement solution in your company you really do need to understand some of the technical choices that have to be made in the process of defining exactly how it should work so that your IT professionals can give you a system which provides you with what you need.

When you have to make choices in construction of a customer profitability measurement model the first question you should ask is why you can't have both alternatives available to you. For example, there is no reason that a customer profitability system can't give you both cash and accrual bases of measurement simultaneously. Similarly you can have different bases of costing available for analysis – if you store sufficient detail and specify the requirements for the model properly. Best in class solutions for Customer Profitability enable you to report on many different bases by storing the detail at a level that allows you choice of what to include at the reporting end of the process rather than at the calculation end.

The key thing to remember in all of this is that the decisions that you as a business manager must make are what should drive the specification of how customer profitability should be measured. You need a clear understanding of your position on these measurement issues to guide the work of your Finance and IT partners to make the measurement model useful to you.

About Customer Profitability measurement systems

If you have been reading this series from the beginning, you will now have an appreciation of some of the complexities that can be involved in implementing a customer profitability measurement method in your business. In this article we offer some relief to concerns you may have about the apparent complexity of the task.

What do you need to get started?

At a minimum you need to have an understanding of what you mean by a "customer" (see Part One: What is Customer Profitability and Why Should We Measure It?) and data that reflects the business you do with your customer.

Before we do a deep dive into the data and technology aspects of it, there are two other requirements that are absolutely imperative to a successful customer profitability measurement implementation project: executive sponsorship and clear statement of purpose.

Executive sponsorship

Except in those rare cases where all of the resources required for implementing a system can be gathered together and devoted to a major undertaking for a long time without interruption, executive sponsorship is a prerequisite to this undertaking.

The amount of time, money and cross-functional coordination that is needed to make a project of this type work demands the involvement of at least one champion executive within your organization. It is better still if you can arrange for the stewardship and sponsorship of the project to be managed by a committee of executives, since this will assure sponsor stability over the long run, which is indeed the investment time frame for a project of this nature.

Plan on a need for uninterrupted sponsorship support over a course of two or three years to ensure that the customer profitability gets physically implemented, supported through its growing pains and becomes an entrenched part of your company's management processes. This is a commitment you really need before you get going.

Statement of purpose

All too often projects involving a lot of IT work are considered to be failures because there is no relevant basis for judging the extent of their success. Customer profitability projects run this very risk.

At the end of the day, what you get as a result of implementing a system is a lot more data about customers, based on data you already had. The technical side of the system is essentially a very big calculator - not very exciting.

What we need is to get at this project's raison d'être - what will you do differently in your company when you have the information? We gave you some ideas about this in the first article of this series, (see Part One: What is Customer Profitability and Why Should We Measure It?). Now is the time to revisit them and put together a clear, well articulated statement of why you are doing this project.

Some companies use customer profitability to add a dimension to segmentation as a means to allocate customer care. Others use it to identify the characteristics of customers they want to acquire, retain or grow relationships with. A few even establish operational objectives and scorecard objectives based on achieving customer profitability based goals. You must know what you want to do differently in your business in order to get value from implementing a system of this type.

Once you've got your statement of purpose together and have your sponsoring executive excited about the project, you are ready to consider the scope of your first implementation. The extent of reliable data, the complexity of your business and your budget are important constraints on how sophisticated your approach should be. Let's take a look at each of these constraints in turn.

Data matters

This topic really breaks down into two discussions - the content of data and whether or not it is reliable. In this section we'll take a look first at the content you may need and then offer some guidelines on data quality you may find useful.

What data do we need?

No matter how simple or complex your business is you need to have three things available to get started:

1. Some way of tracking volume and price (usually transactions or account balances)
2. A way of matching volume and price to customers (a CIF) and
3. Some information about how your business' costs behave.

Without 1 & 2 you really can't begin. If you don't have the ability to "see" volume of activity and link it directly to customers in your data, your infrastructure is not yet developed enough to consider a customer profitability project.

1001 Reasons to love binary

Fortunately most companies with data marts have little or no problem meeting those first level requirements. It is usually the third item - how costs behave - that give people grief. The main reason for the angst is that costing is not something that is exactly measured in any company and it is never precise enough to be considered "right". Costing, by its very nature involves allocating the costs of inputs (people, systems and facilities) to outputs (activities, processes, products or services). Because the inputs rarely match up with the outputs on a one-to-one basis, there is a combination of art and science involved in matching inputs and outputs up through allocations of one type or another.

Matching the costing prepared by your finance group to the data available in your data mart is one of the larger challenges when implementing customer profitability measurement. At a minimum, you should be able to determine the direct cost of the goods or services you have sold in a given transaction.

Beyond that, the merit of increasing the level of cost inclusion to consider alternate channels of distribution and differences in customer behavior is a matter of judgment, which you will need to work out through a dialogue between marketing, who will be the main users of the information produced and finance, who have a wealth of knowledge about how the business works in costing terms. We offer a framework for making this decision based on the nature of your business in the "Complexity of your business" section a little later in this article.

What do we mean by "reliable"

There is no point in building sensitive and sophisticated models on data that is not clean, complete and reliable. We liken this to the foundation of the house - it should be pretty darn solid, if not bedrock; sand will simply not do.

There are some basic checks that should be in place to ensure that your data is good enough.

First and foremost, it should be *complete* - all of the customers (that you are interested in) and all of their transaction, balances or other statistics that will be used as "drivers" (independent variables) in calculations should be present and refreshed reliably in the data. Equally important is to ensure that the relationship between customers and their business activity is complete.

Secondly, it should be *accurate* - values you wish to rely on should be balanced to authoritative sources to ensure that they reasonably reflect the business.

Third, the data you are going to use must be *valid* - not full of blanks, nulls, zeros or odd values that don't make sense.

Finally, the data must be *presented consistently*, for example date formats and number formats from different systems need to made consistent.

These characteristics and checks on data are usually already present in a well implemented data mart or data warehouse. Nonetheless since the customer profitability measurement is such a sensitive calculation (it will be used to change customer treatment, offers etc.) we recommend checking the data you will rely on as a first step - always. Fortunately you are unlikely to use most of the data available in a data mart for this purpose, so you can safely limit your testing and confirmation of data to those elements that you are going to use.

Complexity of your business

Depending on your business, a meaningful measurement of customer profitability can vary from something as simple as the revenue earned on a transaction to the highly complex measurement of customer equity. Choosing the right level of model should be driven by an understanding of the complexity of your business.

What we mean by complexity in this context is how uncertain revenue and cost streams are. Let's take a look at some examples that might help to clarify what we mean.

Level 1: The lemonade stand

The simplest of simple cases is where your company sells one product, with a fixed margin, using the same process every time. To create a useful customer profitability measurement for this business all we really need to do is measure revenue and add it up by customer. The only thing that will differentiate one customer from another is their volume of sales, so all we really need to know is sales dollars. Unfortunately nobody's business is that simple.

Level 2: The variety store

The next level of complexity involves variable margins. Sales mix will affect the profitability of individual customers differently when:

- You offer more than one product or service with different margins
- Prices vary over time or
- Costs vary over time.

Most retail businesses fit into this category. Measuring margin (revenue less direct cost of goods/services sold) at the customer level provides the differentiation we need to differentiate among our customers on the basis of profitability.

Level 3: The "clicks and mortar" store

Alternative channels of distribution increase complexity one more level by making the cost of selling and service delivery transaction specific. In a business with multiple channels of distribution like the web and a physical store, the cost of selling and distributing is highly dependent on the channel of distribution. It is at this point that we need to consider customer behavior (beyond purchase volume) for the first time. It not only matters how much of what our customer buys but also how they buy it. We need to consider selling and distribution costs associated with customer behavior to differentiate properly among our customers.

Level 4: The sales and service organization

The most complex situation we have to deal with is when the customer's use of our product or service is also variable. For example, in a bank or telephone company, individual customers will have widely variable service use patterns. To differentiate among them, we need to introduce further measurements of customer behavior into the profitability equation.

From these examples you can see that customer profitability can and should mean different things to different people. If your business is very simple in structure, it can be modeled in a very simple way to get you the information you need. If your business is complex, more sophisticated approaches will offer you greater precision of understanding.

Help! I'm on a budget!

So, you might ask, can I start simple and get more sophisticated as I go forward? The answer to this is a resounding YES. Increasing the level of sophistication of your customer profitability measurement system is something that can be done over time. The best models are often built starting with simpler revenue-related measures and progressing to more sophisticated views as time, budget and organizational learning permits.

There are some important things to consider here:

- There is no merit in overbuilding a model beyond the complexity inherent in the business.
- Your confidence in decision making based on the output of your model should be proportional to the extent of precision in your measurement.
- Some information is better than no information.

You can start with very little. In some cases six work months of internal resources can produce a good solution. In others, it may take millions of dollars and years to get it right. What is right for your business is a function of what you can afford...what you can't afford is to ignore the value of measuring customer profitability.

Characteristics of a world-class system

In this section we will review the characteristics of a world-class customer profitability measurement system. While it is a daunting list of attributes and features if you are just considering a first implementation, you can take comfort that very few companies today have implemented their measurement capabilities to the extent discussed below. Including them here is intended to give you food for thought when considering what it is you really need.

Precision

Precision is highly variable from implementation to implementation. It depends on accuracy of data, precision of costing algorithms and appropriateness of logic imbedded in business rules which calculate customer profit values.

Precision can be measured in multiple dimensions, reconciling results of customer profitability, geographic profitability and product profitability to authoritative sources such as your management financial statements. Depending on the complexity of your business, you may need to measure only specific items such as revenue or you may need to balance to the bottom line. In companies with the most complex requirements (a bank for example), best in class is typified by revenue precision 100%, costing in excess of 95%, and return on capital (ROC) closely approximating the financials.

Granularity of results

Lowest level of data is always the best level for subsequent analysis. Averages and pooling dilutes the value of the information for analysis purposes.

For example, using average margin for revenue calculations eliminates the possibility of identifying price concessions in any subsequent analysis, since revenue variations become a function of volume alone. Similarly using average costs removes the influence of individual customer behavior from the equation. Many companies also find it useful to know the drivers of costs by type when analyzing results produced by their customer profitability measurement system. If these aspects of customer interaction are important in your business, you will need a system that can support this kind of detail. Measuring revenues and costs - by type - down to the individual account and transaction levels are generally accepted as best in class.

Comparability of results

Comparisons of customers to one another, and to themselves across time periods are central to many of the analytics functions that use customer profitability. Achieving consistency across both customers and time is made difficult by changes in business structure, costing factors, data content (e.g. Household composition) and system changes.

Best in class systems accommodate multiple views to enhance comparability. For example it may be necessary to support current cost factors as well as historical cost factors in the model to ensure that changes in costing practice do not have an impact on the analysis of values being compared.

Flexibility of system design

Additional products and services, calculation methods, allocation methods, sources of data and the like need to be accommodated swiftly, without disruption to production cycles. System design should support rapid update and all sources of input to the calculation process as well as the calculation logic of the system.

Best in class systems offer table driven logic components that can be altered and initialized without extensive amounts of IT involvement. Changes typically need to be supported within one processing cycle.

Timeliness of reporting and change implementation

There are two components to this part: operational cycle and maintenance cycle. The first addresses how often and quickly the customer value calculations are executed; the latter deals with change management.

Operational cycle

Most implementations are monthly. Some are on more frequent (weekly or daily) cycles but this is rare. To date we do not know of any near real time implementations.

Key requirement is that the process runs reliably and within a bounded period of time after data cutoff. It is very important that results be available to other applications such as campaign management, profiling, analytics and even Finance on committed dates each cycle.

Best in class systems typically process overnight after receipt of data and have explicit operational cycles to control dependencies.

Maintenance cycle

Maintenance of business rules (calculation logic), data sources and values such as unit costs used in calculations involve a tradeoff between consistency of information and rapid response to changes in the business.

From a system perspective, there is a need to support rapid changes to the model through table updates, a Graphical User Interface (GUI) and the like to effect changes virtually on demand. Appropriate security controls are required to enable proper management of these sensitive functions.

Best practices in systems include GUI interfaces for updates, standard data interfaces and appropriate security controls to govern maintenance processes.

Time series results

Results produced by profitability measurement systems are often viewed in various time frames. It is highly typical to produce a periodic result each time the system runs. Most companies also retain these results in time-series to enable various smoothing calculations to be effected (e.g. rolling X month averages). Extensive time series storage is supported by today's leading systems.

Versioning of business rules

Dealing with inconsistencies in business logic and data content is imperative to providing meaningful time series analysis. At the same time it may often be useful for a business to look at its customers in different ways such as using actual costs (which agree to the financials) versus standard costs (which remove the influence variations in volume and inputs on unit costs) depending on the nature of the decision management is considering.

The conflict between consistency of measurements over time and the desire to stay up to date (or have alternative views co-exist) is frequently an important consideration when designing or selecting a customer profitability measurement system. Instead of building two different measurement systems to achieve these co-existing views, you may need a system that can provide more than one version of calculations at the same time.

Providing for variety of models simultaneously is a feature not widely supported in commercially available systems. Best in breed systems support unlimited versioning of results.

What if? Analysis based on results

This is an often debated function when it comes to customer profitability systems. The basic idea is that people want to know what effect a change in an assumption or calculation would have on the outcomes. This is typically a consideration when doing a price analysis for example. The two schools of thought presently are either (a) scenarios should be modeled within the system, or (b) scenarios should be modeled outside the system using other tools.

If the extent of processing required is not extensive and there is a need for extensive analysis of results on various different bases e.g. product, customer, geography etc., scenarios can be a very useful function within a system.

In many cases, however scenarios are really just being run to explore a simple question such as what is the effect on revenue of bumping up prices 5%. If this is all that is needed simpler models will prove more cost effective.

Best in class systems may provide this functionality. Consider carefully whether or not your analysis requirements are such that this is really a necessary feature within your business environment before limiting your choice of systems based on this requirement.

Scalability of the system

Over time you may find that you wish to implement customer profitability measurement over a wider base of customers because of growth in your customer base or extension of the system to other divisions of your business. If this is likely to happen in your company, you should be considering the scalability of the system you build or buy at the outset. Best in class customer profitability systems can be scaled to any volume by adding more hardware resources (disk space & processing power) to your technology platform.

Conclusion

In this article we have shown that starting out on the road to customer profitability measurement does not necessarily mean that you have to have a huge budget and all of the information that would be required to produce a financial statement on a customer basis.

Depending on the degree of complexity inherent in your business a relatively simple system might provide you with all the value you might get from implementing a far more sophisticated and complex system.

If your business needs are more complex we have provided a set of criteria you might use when assessing your requirements by setting out the characteristics of a world class customer profitability system, highlighting best in class capabilities available today.

As a final note to this discussion we want to remind you that the value you will derive from implementing a customer profitability system flows from what you will do differently once you have the information. Clearly understanding the intended uses of the information and acquiring executive sponsorship to pursue the strategic investment are important keys to a successful - and rewarding - system implementation.

Managing Customer Profitability measurement systems

Managing is one of the challenges that are often overlooked when planning a project of this nature, yet it is likely the critical success factor that you have the most control over. In this last article of our four part series about Customer Profitability, we are going to share our point of view about how you can best manage the people side of this kind of project rather than the technical and strategy aspects we talked about earlier.

People are what will ultimately make or break the successful implementation of Customer Profitability in your company. From the executive level to your customer facing staff, across several functional areas people will need to be involved if you are going to get real benefit from your Customer Profitability investment.

As the initiative progresses, different groups of people will need to get involved, and the roles of key players will evolve over time. In this article we offer some guidance on how you can manage these changing players and roles. We will begin by looking at who is involved during implementation and will then move on to talk about how to manage the administration of a mature implementation.

Implementation

Whether your business is large or small, simple or complex, implementing Customer Profitability will likely break down into these phases:

Figure 5: Phases of implementation

Development
1. Development of executive sponsorship
2. Development of statement of purpose
3. Development of scope / requirements
4. Assessment of infrastructure capabilities
5. System analysis, design, construction and testing

Deployment
6. Acceptance and analysis of results
7. Designing new business strategies
8. Designing new business tactics
9. Implementing tactics
10. Measuring results

Development

The development process is basically that which any IT project should go through: the traditional Systems Development Life Cycle (SDLC). Customer Profitability is not "just another" IT project, however, because it needs to draw on so many people from different parts of the organization to make it work well. Let's take a few moments to review the "Who-does-what" table below, looking at each stage of the process in turn.

Figure 6: Roles in Development phase

Key Activities	Marketing	Sales	Service	Finance	Specialty Areas	Information Technology
Executive Sponsorship	At least one must sponsor					
Statement of Purpose	At least one must own					
Scope / Requirements	Provide subject matter expertise					Lead
Infrastructure Capabilities				Secure funding		Assess and define
Analysis, Design, Construct and Test	Refine requirements and perform user acceptance tests					Lead

Executive sponsorship

As the chart indicates, the sponsoring executive of a Customer Profitability project can come from any of several functions. In our experience, this leadership role is most often assumed by Marketing or Finance.

We believe that it is important for sponsorship of the project to be anchored in the business functions of the company, rather than your Information Technology (IT) department. There are a variety of reasons for this. First and perhaps most important is that the sponsor of the project should represent an area in the organization that will derive business benefit from implementing it: risks taken to sponsor the project should reside with those who hope to reap the rewards of success. This helps to ensure that goal congruence is maintained throughout the development cycle as tough decisions have to be made about scope, method and content.

As an alternative to a single sponsor, many organizations strike a Steering Committee representing each of several business departments which have a vested interest in the outcome of the project. For example the project might be sponsored by a steering committee made up of Marketing, Finance and IT, ensuring that negotiations between stakeholders with conflicting views or needs are appropriately engaged.

The best approach to take depends largely on the individual people on your management team, and the culture of your company. The people you want sponsoring this project are those that have a clear understanding of why you are doing it. They also need to appreciate the scope of work that needs to be done, be able to partner effectively with other functional areas and last (not least) have a genuine passion for the success of the project.

Statement of purpose

Crafting the Statement of Purpose is clearly something that must come from the business side of the house. In our view, IT and Finance departments are key participants in the process but they are not the business functions who stand to benefit from implementing customer profitability measurement.

For this initiative to have the prominent and sustained executive support that is really needed to implement change in the business based on customer profitability information, there is no substitute for having the business departments that are supposed to benefit from it stand up for the benefits that they will reap right at the beginning.

Your IT and Finance departments shouldn't be shut out of the process, however – they have great experience with articulating statements of benefits from their routine work either preparing or evaluating business case proposals. Partner with these folks to gain the benefit of their expertise and you stand a much better chance of defining the goals of the project in a way that will serve you well down the road.

Scope / requirements

Defining the scope and requirements of the solution is probably the most difficult part of a customer profitability project. During this phase your team will have to determine exactly what you want in terms specific enough that your partners in IT and Finance can commit to helping you implement. Getting the scope and requirements right is crucial: you are determining the standard that success will be measured by.

In this stage of the project there is really no substitute for gathering as much expertise together and working as long as it takes to figure out exactly what you want to end up with. Each of the staff functions in your company has something to contribute that will help you identify opportunities, challenges and shape your expectations.

Remember that actually developing a tool that will compute the profitability of your customers is just the first step in implementation. Your definition of scope and requirements should also define the changes in business practices that you expect to implement. You need to consider the requirements of changes that may be required to systems used for customer contact management, point of sale, rewards (loyalty) programs, campaign design and tracking and others, depending on the business purpose of your implementation. Your IT people can be enormously helpful identifying dependencies that you should be thinking of.

Perhaps even more important than identifying system changes is the impact that changing business practices may have on people. You may need a plan to effect changes in marketing methods, sales and service practices and even your operations. Ensuring that education, training and enthusiasm-building activities are woven into your plan can substantially improve the quality of your success. Human Resources departments are often best suited to identify these types of requirements.

Assessment of infrastructure capabilities

Most companies face limitations in budget, data, technology or people resources which make some of their customer profitability requirements impractical if not impossible to implement. It is necessary to investigate and confirm the resources that you can marshal before development activities begin. Compromising the original requirements based on what can get done with your resources is usually an iterative process, discovering issues, finding work-arounds and modifying requirements until a feasible solution can be specified.

Your IT department should be able to assess the extent of data and technology resources they can support. If you need external help to make this assessment you should get it: unknowns in this area can result in "surprises" down the road which can cause serious overruns in your budget, timeline or both.

Your Finance people will need to get involved to add their expertise as well. They are your internal experts on accounting methods and the drivers of revenue and cost. At this stage, you will need to figure out how revenue and cost drivers are represented in the data and how the accounting methods will be applied to the data. Seek outside help if you don't have the resources or expertise to define this properly.

Specialized expertise from people in Risk, Operations, Sales Human Resources or other departments may also be required to flesh out your requirements into a solution that is defined specifically enough to be constructed.

This phase of the project is often the victim of "scope creep", where new requirements and conflicting alternatives arise as your infrastructure capabilities are matched up with the requirements of your customer profitability implementation. Coordinating and negotiating the perspectives of the functional groups involved is a substantial challenge. You should have a skilled Project Manager driving the progress of the initiative through this phase. In most companies, the best project management skills are found in the IT department, because they work on a project basis all the time. Working to a plan with a known timetable reduces the level of uncertainty for and clarifies the role of each of the departmental groups you will be seeking help from, making it easier for them to contribute effectively.

Analysis, Design, Construction and Testing

If you execute the preceding steps well, this is actually the easiest part of your whole implementation process. At this point the project takes on the shape of a classic system development project, led by your IT department:

Figure 7: Traditional SDLC

To ensure that technical decisions that need to be made are aligned with the requirements as much as possible:

- Sponsorship of the project should remain with the original sponsoring business department,
- Review and approval of analysis and design specifications should be undertaken by areas that contributed to the definition of requirements, and
- User acceptance testing should be performed by end-user departments.

Deployment

Deploying customer profitability in your company means making changes to the way things are done which directly affect customers. Responsibility for making these changes rests with the sponsors of the initiative, usually Marketing, Sales and Service areas of the company. Acceptance of the validity of the information and management of change are two big challenges you are likely to encounter.

Acceptance

Before you can start to make changes affecting customers you should spend some time analyzing and understanding what the new information that customer profitability measurement provides. At a minimum the relationship between the information produced on a customer basis and the financials of your company should be understood before you "go public" with the results. The numbers may not agree – but you had best be able to explain why.

We frequently see companies spend as much as a year questioning and analyzing this information before it is fully accepted and considered to be reliable enough to take actions. Your acceptance period may be shorter or longer, but it is a necessary process: people throughout the company must believe that the information and insight you glean from customer profitability is valid or they will resist change.

Gaining an understanding of exactly how the profitability measurement works and what its results mean usually takes a considerable amount of specialized knowledge and time. Because the investment in learning is high, it is often impractical to spread this knowledge widely within a company. We often see a Centre of Expertise (COE) set up within the Marketing department as the "home" of the specialized knowledge required. These people then serve as a central service point providing analysis and answers to questions that arise company wide. Your best approach is really dependent on the capabilities within your company.

Change

Once your "buy-in" is complete and results have been analyzed and understood you can begin to identify and deploy new strategies and tactics which make gain leverage from customer profitability insights.

The COE can provide information to analysts and strategists, and should participate in the development of ideas, business cases and measurement of program success.

Marketing usually leads this phase of implementation, often working with Sales, Service and Operations leaders. Human Resources or change management SMEs are often brought in to help break down organizational barriers and cultural traditions that impede strategic change.

Maintenance and Enhancement

The investment in measuring customer profitability never really stops. As time goes on you will inevitably find better ways of measuring and deploying customer profitability as your infrastructure develops and you learn more about how customer behavior and marketing actions affect customer profitability.

After initial deployment significantly less work and breadth of coordination is required to keep the system and infrastructure working well. Nonetheless you will need to dedicate some resources to ensure that your customer profitability measurement keeps pace with change in the company. As you add new products, convert systems, change accounting policies etc. these changes need to be reflected in your customer profitability measurement.

The COE should manage the change cycle, assigning relative importance to changes required based on their relevance to the business. Change requests should then be routed to IT for estimation of time and cost before a decision is made whether or not to proceed. Matching up the relative priority and cost of requested changes is a process that fits nicely within the COE mandate.

Conclusion

Throughout the implementation of customer profitability measurement in your organization people are the key ingredient to success. Ensuring that you involve the right people at the right time as the project develops is one of the things you can do right to ensure that your implementation delivers on your expectations and requirements within your time and budget constraints.

Marketing often has a central role in all aspects of customer profitability implementation management, because understanding the economic relationship between customers and company is close to the essence of the Marketer's role. Nonetheless you can't do it alone: implementing customer profitability is a project that demands a cross-functional management process to bring the skills and knowledge of almost every part of your company together.

In this series of articles we have introduced ideas about what customer profitability is, why and how to measure it, what a measurement system might look like and how to manage the process of implementation. We have strived to demystify what often appears to be a very complicated topic through a clear framework of discussion. You should now be armed with an informed point of view to share with your colleagues in Marketing and throughout your company. Perhaps you will be the champion of Customer Profitability measurement in your organization, leading the development of valuable customer insight.

www.ingramcontent.com/pod-product-compliance
Lightning Source LLC
Chambersburg PA
CBHW040920180526
45159CB00002BA/548